The Amazing Travels of Magellan the Cardinal

Written and illustrated by Sharon K. Thurow

Published by
Three Towers Press
An imprint of HenschelHAUS Publishing, Inc.
www.henschelHAUSbooks.com
Milwaukee, Wisconsin

ISBN: 979-8-9912791-3-0
LCCN: 2024949559

Printed in the United States

This book is dedicated to my "boys" —

Jason, Michael, Adam and my husband James—who inspired me to write this story about the wonderful animals and their various habitats.

Author's Note

The star of this story, Magellan the Cardinal, was named after a real person named Ferdinand Magellan, a Portuguese explorer, who was born more than 500 years ago. In 1519, Captain Magellan set sail from Spain with five ships to find a westward route to the Spice Islands. Today, the Spice Islands are called the Maluku Islands in Indonesia.

The ships faced many challenges while exploring new place, including very hazardous and dangerous waters. Magellan's expedition led to the southern tip of South America, where they discovered a passage leading from the Atlantic Ocean to the Pacific Ocean—the Straight of Magellan.

These explorations gave us all important information about the earth and the oceans.

Magellan the Cardinal is also an explorer and as he flies around the world, he makes many friends.

I hope that you also have fun learning about the different animals on the six continents and how they live.

The Magellan-Elcano Expedition

1519-1522

Magellan the Cardinal was sitting on a branch of a tree and singing a song of longing to travel the around the world and explore from shore to shore.

Magellan is a songbird from North America and has a black face and bright red body that _radiates_* in the sun.

He is one of the most beautiful feathered friends around as he glides through the air with ease and sings his songs for fun.

* **To radiate**: To stand out or shine.

Magellan took off and flew to the first of six **continents.*** He landed in Africa. He looked around and spotted an aardvark, a bush baby, and a cheetah **wandering**** his way.

***Continent:** Part of the Earth's surface that forms a large land mass. There are six continents: Africa, North America, South America, Australia, Antarctica, and Eurasia. Eurasia is made up of Europe and Asia.

** **To wander**: To move about with no real purpose.

Adam the Aardvark lives in the hot jungles and bright sun of Africa.

He has a nose like a pig and ears like a donkey. He uses his sharp claws to tear at **_termite_*** nests for food. Adam likes to eat termites. He uses his long, sticky tongue to lick up termites. When he is full, he moves on his way.

*Termite: a white-bodied, wood-consuming insect

Bruce the Bush Baby also **_resides_*** in the forests of Africa and grows up to be as big as a cat. Bruce eats grasshoppers, fruits, flowers, and seeds. Bruce is also called a galago.

* **_To reside_**: To live in an area or building.

Charlie the Cheetah is a large cat with many spots.

Charlie lives on the plains of Africa. He grows up to four feet high and is the fastest runner of all animals.

He chases and hunts antelope to eat.

Magellan said goodbye to all of his friends in Africa and flew away in the clouds. He flew to Eurasia, which actually **consist**s of two continents in one: Europe and Asia.

He sang as he flew, and from his height in the clouds, he saw many wonderful sights.

Magellan flew to Eurasia to see new things and discover old ones.

He met a wolf, a beaver, and a monkey as he flew through the forests. He decided to rest for a while, landing close to a nearby pond to rest up for more exciting views.

*To consist of: To be a part of something

Roger the Wolf roams around, sometimes alone and most of the time in small groups called packs. He eats deer, moose, and smaller animals, as well as other snacks. He grows to be 3 feet tall and runs with his friends all day.

Roger uses his senses of sight and smell to find food along the way.

Bucky the Beaver lives along the _streams_ of Asia (and North America) and eats tree bark and water plants.

He cuts down trees with his strong teeth to make new _dams**_ to create ponds. He has a flat tail that he can slap on the water to make a loud noise.

He can grow up to 5 feet in length—maybe as big as you or me.

* _Stream_: A small river

** _Dam_: Barrier built across a stream to create a pond

Maggie the Monkey lives in large groups in the forests and rocky hillsides of South, Central, and Southeast Asia. She eats leaves and fruits, often from gardens and in the wild.

Maggie is clever and active and grows to be around 2 feet tall. When she has babies, she carries them on her body and stays close to them. She **_protects_*** them from falls and from being eaten by birds or other animals.

***_To protect_**: To keep from harm

One morning, Magellan woke up and decided to visit the _island_ continent of Australia. Australia is the only continent to also be a country.

Magellan flew for many hours until he reached the Outback of Australia. That day, he saw a kangaroo, a duck-billed platypus, and even a wombat.

*_Island:_ Land that is surrounded by water

Katelyn the Kangaroo lives in Australia and other islands that are close by.

Kangaroos are **_marsupials_***, which means they carry their babies in a pouch on their bellies.

She carries her baby, called a joey, in her pouch.

Kangaroos can grow to be 7 feet high.

*_Marsupial:_ Animals unique to Australia that raise their babies in a pouch on their bellies.

Wally the Wombat is a **_unique_*** animal that lives mostly underground and digs tunnels during the day. Wally is also a marsupial.

Wombats leave their tunnels at night to find food like grass and roots. They are about 3 feet high and are quite gentle and **_respectful._****

***_Unique:_** One of a kind, unusual.

****_Respectful:_** To look at something or someone in a positive way.

Penny the Duck-billed Platypus is also unique animal of Australia. She is a **_mammal_*** _that has **a**_ duck-like bill, a beaver-like tail, and otter-like feet.

She grows to be about 2 feet long and eats worms, shrimp, and tadpoles.

Unlike other mammals, Penny lays eggs like a **_reptile_**** or bird, instead of giving birth to live young.

***_Mammal_**: Warm-blooded animals that nurse their babies and have hair on their bodies.

****_Reptile_**: Cold-blooded animals like snakes, lizards, and turtles that have cold, scaly skin and lay eggs.

Magellan dreamed of traveling to South America. He flapped his wings as he said, "Good-bye" to his new friends.

He also sang a song of **_gratitude_*** as he flew up high in the sky.

When he arrived on the continent of South America many miles later, he saw a tapir, a sloth, and even a snake. He decided to stay and explore this new land.

*Gratitude: Feeling thankful

Tilly the Tapir lives in the hot jungles of South America. She grows to be about 3 feet tall.

She has 4 toes on her front feet and only 3 toes on her back feet.

Tapirs are large mammals that only eat grass and other plants. They have a long, pig-like snout. They belong to the same ancient family as horses and rhinoceroses.

Sally the Sloth lives in the jungles of South America, like her friend Tilly the Tapir.

She spends most of her time hanging upside down in trees, where she eats leaves.

Sloths are known for being very slow.

Jake the Snake slithers along the ground and has no legs at all.

He moves quite well, zigzagging along, and never has to worry about a fall.

Jake is a Diamond-back Rattlesnake and makes noises called a "rattle" to give warning.

He catches small animals with his poison, swallowing his **prey*** whole. He can grow to be 7 feet long.

***Prey**: When one animal hunts another for food

Magellan knew he needed to fly to the coldest continent as well, Antarctica. It is an island and a continent, like Australia. It is completely covered by ice.

He saw a whale swimming in the distance, quickly going on his way.

Magellan also **_noticed_*** a penguin waddling on the ice and a sled-dog **_frolicking_**** that day.

***_To notice_**: To see someone or something

****_To frolic_**: To play and have fun.

Wally the Whale looks like a big fish,

But is really a mammal, like a cat or a dog.

He has teeth to eat fish, breathes air, and even has hair. Whale babies drink milk from their mothers.

Wally eats fish and seals and can grow very large.

Paul the Penguin is a bird, but unlike Magellan, is unable to fly.

He's a great swimmer and when on land, he waddles from side to side on the ice,

He lives on top of the ice near the South Pole and grows to be about 4 feet tall.

Karra the Husky is a sled dog and is gentle to everyone around.

She is friendly and a good pet and works hard on the cold, icy ground.

Magellan enjoyed his visit to Antarctica and to the other continents, but now it was time to go home. So he said good-bye to Willy, Paul, and Karra and hoped to stay in touch somehow.

Magellan then flew thousands of miles until he reached in home in North America.

On the way, he met some of his friends, Rocky the Racoon, Hector the Turtle, and Wanda the Wolverine.

North America

Rocky the Racoon lives in hollow trees, caves, and other hiding places in the forest.

He eats frogs, snakes, insects, corn, and other food.

Racoons wash their food before eating it.

They can grow up to 3 feet high.

Hector is a Snapping Turtle. He has powerful jaws and can grow to be about 2 feet long.

Turtles are reptiles that live near water and lay eggs.

They are also known for moving very slowly.

Wanda the Wolverine is a fierce fighter with strong jaws. She eats rabbits and other small mammals. Sometimes she even catches deer much larger than she is.

Wolverines are loners. They can grow to be 3 feet long, and hunts by themselves.

Magellan will never forget the new friends he made on his long journey. He would visit them from time to time, but let them know that he could not stay — his home was in North America.

Magellan sang his songs and remembered the many new sights he saw on his travels. Now he was glad to be home again.

About the Author
Sharon Thurow, FNP, BC

Sharon has been a family Nurse Practitioner for over 25 years and a registered nurse for over 24. She attended Deaconess School of Nursing in Milwaukee and received her BSN as well as Masters through Concordia University in Mequon, WI. Sharon was also certified as a critical care nurse by the American Critical Care Nurses Association.

www.ingramcontent.com/pod-product-compliance
Lightning Source LLC
Chambersburg PA
CBHW060911270326
41930CB00004B/109